Sir Noël Coward

His Words And Music

A COLLECTION OF 32 COWARD CLASSICS

BOOK DESIGNED AND EDITED
BY LEE SNIDER

CHAPPELL & CO., INC.
NEW YORK

RANDOM HOUSE
NEW YORK
Exclusive Distributor to the Book Trade

ISBN 0-394-70978-0
Library of Congress Catalog Card Number 73-1154

A special debt of gratitude is expressed to
Mr. Nicholas Firth, Chappell & Co., Inc.
and to Mr. E. C. Holmes, Chappell & Co., Ltd.
for their valuable contributions in preparing
this book.

PHOTO CREDITS

Front Cover: **HORST TAPPE**

P. 4, 154, 160, 170, 171: **FRIEDMAN-ABELES**

P. 172-173: **FRIEDMAN-ABELES (Courtesy Bob Ullman and Warren Pincus)**

P. 7, 33, 64, 110, 111, 146: **CHAPPELL & CO., LTD.**

P. 150: **MONROE MENDELSOHN STUDIOS**

INTRODUCTION
by Sir Noël Coward

I was born into a generation that still took light music seriously. The lyrics and melodies of Gilbert and Sullivan were hummed and strummed into my consciousness at an early age. My father sang them, my mother played them, my nurse, Emma, breathed them through her teeth while she was washing me, dressing me and undressing me and putting me to bed. My aunts and uncles, who were legion, sang them singly and in unison at the slightest provocation. By the time I was four years old 'Take a Pair of Sparkling Eyes', 'Tit Willow', 'We're Very Wide Awake, the Moon and I' and 'I Have a Song to Sing-O' had been fairly inculcated into my bloodstream.

The whole Edwardian era was saturated with operetta and musical comedy: in addition to popular foreign importations by Franz Lehar, Leo Fall, André Messager, etc., our own native composers were writing musical scores of a quality that has never been equalled in this country since the 1914-18 war. Lionel Monckton, Paul Rubens, Ivan Caryll and Leslie Stuart were flourishing. 'The Quaker Girl',

'Our Miss Gibbs', 'Miss Hook of Holland', 'Florodora', 'The Arcadians' and 'The Country Girl', to name only a few, were all fine musical achievements, and over and above the artists who performed them, the librettists who wrote them and the impresarios who presented them, their music was the basis of their success. Their famous and easily remembered melodies can still be heard on the radio and elsewhere, but it was in the completeness of their scores that their real strength lay: opening choruses, finales, trios, quartettes and concerted numbers — all musicianly, all well balanced and all beautifully constructed.

There was no song-plugging in those days beyond an occasional reprise in the last act; there was no assaulting of the ear by monstrous repetition, no unmannerly nagging. A little while ago I went to an American 'musical' in which the hit number was reprised no less than five times during the performance by different members of the cast, as well as being used in the overture, the entr'acte and as a 'play-out' while the audience was leaving the theatre. The other numbers in the show, several of which were charming, were to fend for themselves and only three of them were ever published. In earlier days the complete vocal score of a musical comedy was published as a matter of course, in addition to which a booklet of the lyrics could be bought in the theatre with the programme. These little paper-bound books were well worth the sixpence charged because they helped those with a musical ear to recapture more easily the tunes they wanted to remember and to set them in their minds.

In the years immediately preceding the first world war the American Invasion began innocuously with a few isolated song hits until Irving Berlin established a beach-head with 'Alexander's Ragtime Band'. English composers, taken by surprise and startled by vital Negro-Jewish rhythms from the New World, fell back in some disorder; conservative musical opinion was shocked and horrified by such alien noises and, instead of saluting the new order and welcoming the new vitality, turned up its patrician nose and retired disgruntled from the arena.

At this moment war began, and there was no longer any time. It is reasonable to suppose that a large number of potential young composers were wiped out in those sad years and that had they not been, the annihilation of English light music would not have been so complete. As it was, when finally the surviving boys came home, it was to an occupied country; the American victory was a *fait accompli*. This obviously was the moment for British talent to rally, to profit by defeat, to absorb and utilize the new, exciting rhythms from over the water and to modify and adapt them to its own service, but apparently this was either beyond our capacity or we were too tired to attempt it. At all events, from the nineteen-twenties until today, there have been few English composers of light music capable of creating an integrated score.

One outstanding exception was the late Ivor Novello. His primary talent throughout his whole life was music, and 'Glamorous Night', 'Arc de Triomphe', 'The Dancing Years', 'Perchance to Dream' and 'King's Rhapsody' were rich in melody and technically expert. For years he upheld, almost alone, our old traditions of musical Musical Comedy. His principal tunes were designed, quite deliberately, to catch the ear of the public and, being simple, sentimental, occasionally conventional but always melodic, they invariably achieved their object. The rest of his scores, the openings, finales, choral interludes and incidental themes he wrote to please himself and in these, I believe, lay his true quality; a much finer quality than most people realized. The fact that his music never received the critical acclaim that it deserved was irritating but unimportant. One does not expect present-day dramatic critics to know much about music; as a matter of fact one no longer expects them to know much about drama. Vivian Ellis has also proved over the years that he can handle a complete score with grace and finesse. 'Bless the Bride' was much more than a few attractive songs strung together and so, from the

musical standpoint, was 'Tough at the Top', although the show on the whole was a commercial failure.

Harold Fraser-Simson, who composed 'The Maid of the Mountains' and Frederic Norton, who composed 'Chu Chin Chow', are remembered only for these two outstanding scores. Their other music, later or earlier, is forgotten except by a minority.

I now arrive at the moment when willy-nilly I must discuss, as objectively as possible, my own contributions to this particular field. I have, within the last twenty-five years, composed many successful songs and three integrated scores of which I am genuinely proud. These are 'Bitter Sweet', 'Conversation Piece', and 'Pacific 1860'. 'This Year of Grace' and 'Words and Music', although revues, were also well constructed musically. 'Operette' was sadly meagre with the exception of three numbers, 'Dearest Love', 'Where are the Songs we Sung?' and 'The Stately Homes of England'. This latter, however, being a comedy quartette, relied for its success more on its lyrics than its tune. 'Ace of Clubs' contained several good songs, but could not fairly be described as a musical score. 'Sigh No More', 'On with the Dance' and 'London Calling' are outside this discussion as they were revues containing contributions from other composers. 'Bitter Sweet', the most flamboyantly successful of all my musical shows, had a full and varied score greatly enhanced by the orchestrations of Orrelana. 'Conversation Piece' was less full and varied but had considerable quality. With these two scores Miss Elsie April, to whom I dictated them, was a tremendous help to me both in transcribing and in sound musical advice. 'Pacific 1860' was, musically, my best work to date. It was carefully balanced and well constructed and imaginatively orchestrated by Ronald Binge and Mantovani. The show, as a whole, was a failure. It had been planned on a small scale, but, owing to theatre exigencies and other circumstances, had to be blown up to fit the stage of Drury Lane. The Press blasted the book, hardly mentioned the music or lyrics, and that was that. It closed after a few months.

Proceeding on the assumption that the reader of this preface is interested in the development of my musical talent, I will try to explain, as concisely as I can, how, in this respect, my personal wheels go round. To begin with, I have only had two music lessons in my life. These were the first steps of what was to have been a full course at the Guildhall School of Music, and they faltered and stopped when I was told by my instructor that I could not use consecutive fifths. He went on to explain that a gentleman called Ebenezer Prout had announced many years ago that consecutive fifths were wrong and must in no circumstances be employed. At that time Ebenezer Prout was merely a name to me (as a matter of fact he still is, and a very funny one at that) and I was unimpressed by his Victorian dicta. I argued back that Debussy and Ravel used consecutive fifths like mad. My instructor waved aside this triviality with a pudgy hand, and I left his presence for ever with the parting shot that what was good enough for Debussy and Ravel was good enough for me. This outburst of rugged individualism deprived me of much valuable knowledge, and I have never deeply regretted it for a moment. Had I intended at the outset of my career to devote all my energies to music I would have endured the necessary training cheerfully enough, but in those days I was passionately involved in the theatre; acting and writing and singing and dancing seemed of more value to my immediate progress than counterpoint and harmony. I was willing to allow the musical side of my creative talent to take care of itself. On looking back, I think that on the whole I was right. I have often been irritated in later years by my inability to write music down effectively and by my complete lack of knowledge of orchestration except by ear, but being talented from the very beginning in several different media, I was forced by common sense to make a decision. The decision I made was to try to become a good writer and actor, and to compose tunes and harmonies whenever the urge to do so became too powerful to resist.

I have never been unduly depressed by the fact that all my music has to be dictated. Many famous light composers never put so much as a crotchet* on paper. To be born with a natural ear for music is a great and glorious gift. It is no occasion for pride and it has nothing to do with will-power, concentration or industry. It is either there or it isn't. What is so curious is that it cannot, in any circumstances, be wrong where one's own harmonies are concerned. In New York, when I was recording 'Conversation Piece' with Lily Pons, I detected a false note in the orchestration. It happened to be in a very fully scored passage and the mistake was consequently difficult to trace. The orchestrator, the conductor and the musical producer insisted that I was wrong; only Lily Pons, who has perfect pitch, backed me up. Finally, after much argument and fiddle-faddle it was discovered that the oboe was playing an A flat instead of an A natural. The greatness and gloriousness of this gift, however, can frequently be offset by excruciating discomfort. On many occasions in my life I have had to sit smiling graciously while some well-meaning but inadequate orchestra obliges with a selection from my works. Cascades of wrong notes lacerate my nerves, a flat wind instrument pierces my ear-drums, and though I continue to smile appreciatively, the smile, after a little while, becomes tortured and looks as if my mouth were filled with lemon juice.

I could not help composing tunes even if I wished to. Ever since I was a little boy they have dropped into my mind unbidden and often in the most unlikely circumstances. The 'Bitter Sweet' waltz, 'I'll See You Again', came to me whole and complete in a taxi when I was appearing in New York in 'This Year of Grace'. I was on my way home to my apartment after a matinée and had planned, as usual, to have an hour's rest and a light dinner before the evening performance. My taxi got stuck in a traffic block on the corner of Broadway and Seventh Avenue, klaxons were honking, cops were shouting and suddenly in the general din there was the melody, clear and unmistakable. By the time I got home the words of the first phrase had emerged. I played it over and over again on the piano (key of E flat as usual) and tried to rest, but I was too excited to sleep.

Oddly enough, one of the few songs I ever wrote that came to me in a setting appropriate to its content was 'Mad Dogs and Englishmen'. This was conceived and executed during a two-thousand-mile car drive from Hanoi in Tonkin to the Siamese border.

The birth of 'I'll Follow my Secret Heart' was even more surprising. I was working on 'Conversation Piece' at Goldenhurst, my home in Kent. I had completed some odd musical phrases here and there but no main waltz theme, and I was firmly and miserably stuck. I had sat at the piano daily for hours, repeatedly trying to hammer out an original tune or even an arresting first phrase, and nothing had resulted from my concentrated efforts but banality. I knew that I could never complete the score without my main theme as a pivot and finally, after ten days' increasing despair, I decided to give up and, rather than go on flogging myself any further, postpone the whole project for at least six months. This would entail telegraphing to Yvonne Printemps who was in Paris waiting eagerly for news and telling Cochran who had already announced the forthcoming production in the Press. I felt fairly wretched but at least relieved that I had had the sense to admit failure while there was still time. I poured myself a large whisky and soda, dined in grey solitude, poured myself another, even larger, whisky and soda, and sat gloomily envisaging everybody's disappointment and facing the fact that my talent had withered and that I should never write any more music until the day I died. The whisky did little to banish my gloom, but there was no more work to be done and I didn't care if I became fried as a coot, so I gave myself another drink and decided to go to bed. I switched off the lights at the door and noticed that there was one lamp left on by the piano. I walked automatically to turn it off, sat down and played 'I'll Follow my Secret Heart', straight through in E flat, a key I had never played in before.

*quarter-note

There is, to me, strange magic in such occurrences. I am willing and delighted to accept praise for my application, for my self-discipline and for my grim determination to finish a thing once I have started it. My acquired knowledge is praiseworthy, too, for I have worked hard all my life to perfect the material at my disposal. But these qualities, admirable as they undoubtedly are, are merely accessories. The essential talent is what matters and essential talent is unexplainable. My mother and father were both musical in a light, amateur sense, but their gift was in no way remarkable. My father, although he could improvise agreeably at the piano, never composed a set piece of music in his life. I have known many people who were tone-deaf whose parents were far more actively musical than mine. I had no piano lessons when I was a little boy except occasionally from my mother who tried once or twice, with singular lack of success, to teach me my notes. I could, however, from the age of about seven onwards, play any tune I had heard on the piano in the pitch dark. To this day my piano-playing is limited to three keys: E flat, B flat and A flat. The sight of two sharps frightens me to death.

When I am in the process of composing anything in the least complicated I can play it in any key on the keyboard, but I can seldom if ever repeat these changes afterwards unless I practise them assiduously every day. In E flat I can give the impression of playing well. A flat and B flat I can get away with, but if I have to play anything for the first time it is always to my beloved E flat that my fingers move automatically. Oddly enough, C major, the key most favoured by the inept, leaves me cold. It is supposed to be easier to play in than any of the others because it has no black notes, but I have always found it dull. Another of my serious piano-playing defects is my left hand.

Dear George Gershwin used to moan at me in genuine distress and try to force my fingers on to the right notes. As a matter of fact he showed me a few tricks that I can still do, but they are few and dreadfully far between. I can firmly but not boastfully claim that I am a better pianist than Irving Berlin, but as that superlative genius of light music is well known not to be able to play at all except in C major, I will not press the point. Jerome D. Kern, to my mind one of the most inspired romantic composers of all, played woodenly as a rule and without much mobility. Dick Rodgers plays his own music best when he is accompanying himself or someone else, but he is far from outstanding. Vincent Youmans was a marvellous pianist, almost as brilliant as Gershwin, but these are the only two I can think of who, apart from their creative talent, could really play.

At the very beginning of this introduction I said that I was born into a generation that took light music seriously. It was fortunate for me that I was, because by the time I had emerged from my teens the taste of the era had changed. In my early twenties and thirties it was from America that I gained my greatest impetus. In New York they have always taken light music seriously. There, it is, as it should be, saluted as a specialized form of creative art, and is secure in its own right. The basis of a successful American musical show is now and has been for many years its music and its lyrics. Here in England there are few to write the music and fewer still to recognize it when it is written. The commercial managers have to fill their vast theatres and prefer, naturally enough, to gamble on acknowledged Broadway successes rather than questionable home products. The critics are quite incapable of distinguishing between good light music and bad light music, and the public are so saturated with the cheaper outpourings of Tin Pan Alley, which are dinned into their ears interminably by the B.B.C., that their natural taste will soon die a horribly unnatural death. It is a depressing thought, but perhaps some day soon, someone, somewhere, will appear with an English musical so strong in native quality that it will succeed in spite of the odds stacked against it.

NOËL COWARD and **GERTRUDE LAWRENCE,** a team "born to amuse"

CONTENTS

Dance, Little Lady

"THIS YEAR OF GRACE"

NOËL COWARD

Refrain Eb
Allegretto

Dance, dance, dance, lit - tle la - dy! Youth is fleet-

- ing to the rhy - thm beat - ing in your

mind. _____ Dance, dance, dance, lit - tle la - dy!

So ob - sessed _ with sec - ond best, no rest _ you'll ev - er

dance, lit - tle la - dy! Leave your troub - les be -

hind.

hind.

A Room With A View

"THIS YEAR OF GRACE"

Noël Coward

Moderato

mf

p

I've been cher-ish-ing Through the per-ish-ing win-ter nights and

days A fun-ny lit-tle phrase, That means

World Weary

NOËL COWARD

"THIS YEAR OF GRACE"

When I'm feel-ing drear-y and blue I'm on-ly too glad to be left a-lone,
Get up in the morn-ing at eight, Re-lent-less Fate Drives me to work at nine;

Dream-ing of a place in the sun when day— is done,
Toil-ing like a bee in a hive From four— to five,

Far from a tel-e-phone; Bus-tle and the wear-y crowd,
Wheth-er it's wet or fine, Hard-ly ev-er see the sky,

If Love Were All

"BITTER SWEET"

NOËL COWARD

REFRAIN (plaintively)

"Bitter Sweet" (1929) - PEGGY WOOD and GEORGE METAXA sing "I'll See You Again"

I'll See You Again

"BITTER SWEET"

NOËL COWARD

Zigeuner

"BITTER SWEET"

NOËL COWARD

Tempo di Valse

Once up-on a time,_____ Man-y years a-go_____
_____ Lived a fair Prin-cess Hat-ing to con-fess Lone-li-ness was

Someday I'll Find You

"PRIVATE LIVES"

NOËL COWARD

But never ap - pear. Each night I
Why should - n't we meet? When you're a -

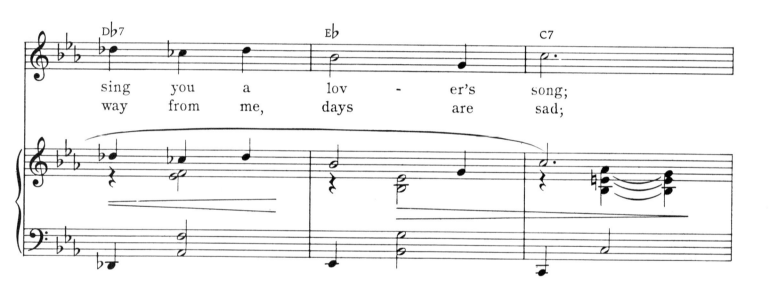

sing you a lov - er's song;
way from me, days are sad;

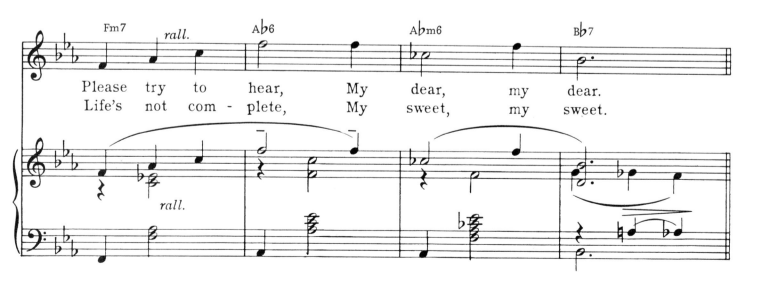

Please try to hear, My dear, my dear.
Life's not com - plete, My sweet, my sweet.

Let's Say Goodbye

"WORDS AND MUSIC"

NOËL COWARD

Now we've em-bark'd on this love af-fair, Don't let's des-troy it with tears,_____ Once we be-gin To let

Mad About The Boy

NOËL COWARD

"WORDS AND MUSIC"

Mad Dogs And Englishmen

Noël Coward

"WORDS AND MUSIC"

The Party's Over Now

Noël Coward

"WORDS AND MUSIC"

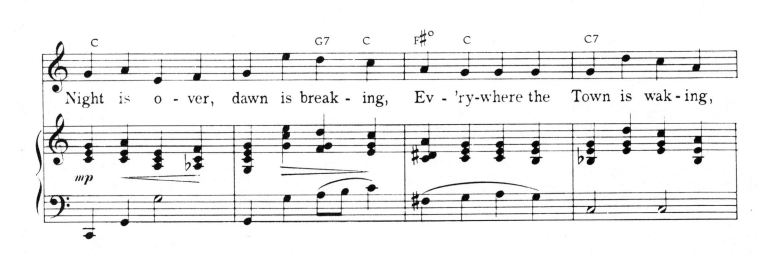

Night is o - ver, dawn is break - ing, Ev - 'ry-where the Town is wak - ing,

Just as we are on our way to sleep.

WORDS AND MUSIC (1932)

Top, Ivy St. Helier, Gerald Nodin, and Romney Brent

At left, Joyce Barbour and Chorus

CONVERSATION PIECE (1934)

Louis Hayward, Yvonne Printemps, Noël Coward, and Irene Browne

I'll Follow My Secret Heart

"CONVERSATION PIECE"

NOËL COWARD

Don't Put Your Daughter On The Stage,
Mrs. Worthington

noël coward

Allegro moderato (*nice and breezy*)

PIANO

Don't put your daugh-ter on the stage, Mis-sis Worth-ing-ton;

Don't put your daugh-ter on the stage._____ The pro-

Play, Orchestra, Play

"TONIGHT AT 8:30"

NOËL COWARD

PIANO

Lis-ten to the strain, it plays once more for us,

There it is a-gain The past in store for us.

Has Anybody Seen Our Ship?

Noël Coward

"TONIGHT AT 8:30"

"What shall we do with the
What shall be done with the

drunk - en Sail - or?" So the say - ing goes.
girls on shore who lead our tars a - stray?

We're not tight but we're none too bright, Great Scott! I don't sup-
What's to be done with the drinks ga - lore That

pose. We've lost our way and we've lost our pay and to
way? We got wet ears from our first five beers, af - ter

make the thing com - plete We've been and gone and
that we lost con - trol And now we find we're

lost the bloom - ing fleet.
up the blink - ing pole.

Men About Town

NOËL COWARD

"TONIGHT AT 8:30"

We're two chaps who find it thrill-ing to do the kill-ing, we're al-ways will-ing to give the girls a treat._____ Just a drink at the Ritz,

We Were Dancing

Noël Coward

"TONIGHT AT 8:30"

Tempo di Valse

If you can ___ i - ma - gine my em - bar - rass - ment when you po - lite - ly ask me to ex - plain man to man, ___ I can - not help, but

You Were There

"TONIGHT AT 8:30"

Noël Coward

Was__ it in the real world? Or was__ it in a dream?
How__ could we ex - plain it, The spark__ and then the fire?

Was__ it just a note__ in some e - ter - nal theme?
How__ add up the to - tal of our heart's de - sire?

The Stately Homes Of England

Noël Coward

"OPERETTE"

pro - ducts of those homes se - rene and state - ly____ Which on - ly
some - times flaunt our fam - i - ly con - ven - tions,____ Our good in -

late - ly____ Seem to have run to seed!____ The
ten - tions____ Must - n't be mis - con - strued.____ The

REFRAIN

State - ly Homes of Eng - land How beau - ti - ful they stand,_ To prove the up - per
State - ly Homes of Eng - land We proud - ly re - pre - sent,_ We on - ly keep them

class - es Have still the up - per hand; Tho' the fact that they have to be re - built And
up for A - mer - i - cans to rent. Tho' the pipes that sup - ply the bath room burst And the

We Must All Be Very Kind To
Auntie Jessie

Noël Coward

OPERETTE (1938), Kenneth Carten, Ross Landon, John Gattrell, and Hugh French sing "The Stately Homes Of England"

TONIGHT AT 8:30, Noël Coward and Gertrude Lawrence perform "Has Anybody Seen Our Ship?" (1936)

Right, Bea Lillie and Richard Haydn in SET TO MUSIC (1939)

BEA LILLIE sings "I Went To A Marvelous Party" from "Set To Music" (1939)

I Went To A Marvelous Party

Noël Coward

"SET TO MUSIC"

Quite for no rea - son I'm here for the sea - son, And

high as a kite. Liv - ing in er - ror With

shells and a black feath-er boa.____ Poor Mill - i -cent wore a sur-

re - al - ist comb Made of bits of Mo - saic from St.

Pe - ter's in Rome, But the weight was so great that she had to go home, I

could - n't have liked it more!____ I've more!____

Three White Feathers

"SET TO MUSIC"

Noël Coward

I can't help feel - ing
By eas - y sta - ges

Fate's made a fool of me
Though my be - gin - nings were

rath - er,
hum - ble,

It's placed me where I should-n't be And
I've stud - ied each small move - ment Of my

London Pride

Noël Coward

fruit piled high. Woa Li - za lit - tle Lon - don spar - rows
lone - ly beat. Gay la - dy May - fair in the morn - ing

Cov - ent Gar - den Mar - ket where the cos - ters cry. Cock - ney feet, mark the
Hear the foot - steps ech - o in the emp - ty street. Ear - ly rain and the

poco rit.   *a tempo*

beat of his - to - ry Ev - 'ry street pins a mem - o - ry down.
pave - ments glist - en - ing All Park Lane in a shim - mer - ing gown.

Noth - ing ev - er can quite re - place The grace of Lon - don Town.
Noth - ing ev - er could break or harm The charm of Lon - don Town.

Stay cit-y smok-i-ly en-chant-ed Cra-dle of our mem-o-ries and hopes and fears Ev-'ry Blitz your re-sis-tance tough-en-ing From the Ritz to the An-chor and Crown, Noth-ing ev-er could o-ver ride The pride of Lon-don Town.

Matelot

"SIGH NO MORE"

Noël Coward

Nina

"SIGH NO MORE"

NOËL COWARD

132

This Is A Changing World

"PACIFIC 1860"

NOËL COWARD

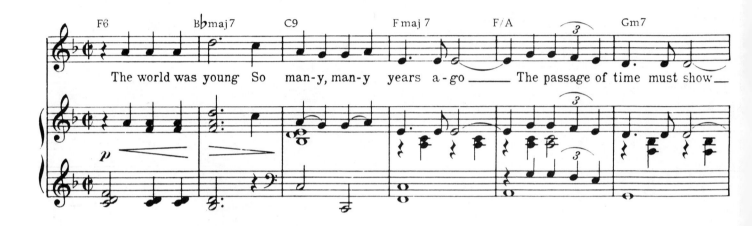

The world was young So man-y, man-y years a-go____ The passage of time must show

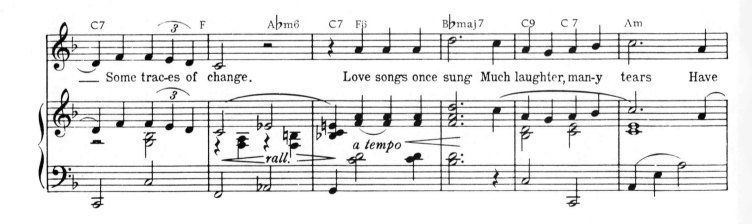

____ Some trac-es of change. Love songs once sung Much laughter, man-y tears Have

ech-oed down the years, The past is old and strange.____ Each wan-ing

Chase Me, Charlie

"ACE OF CLUBS"

NOËL COWARD

Bright Valse tempo

PIANO

1. When it's late ____ and the world is sleep - ing,
2. Ev - 'ry night at a - bout e - lev - en,

Our lit - tle black cat, No big - ger than that,
Our lit - tle cat knows, Our lit - tle cat goes,

Above, Night Club Scene from ACE OF CLUBS (1950)

At right, SIGH NO MORE (1945) with Madge Elliott and Cyril Ritchard

Below, Elaine Stritch demonstrates The Little Ones' ABC in SAIL AWAY (1961)

Sail Away

"SAIL AWAY"

NOËL COWARD

A dif-f'rent sky, New worlds to gaze up-on,

The strange ex-cite-ment of an un-fa-mil-iar shore.

One more good-bye, One more il-lu-sion gone,

ELAINE STRITCH and NOËL COWARD confer during a "Sail Away" rehearsal (1961)

Opening Night souvenir program. Illustration by Mr. Coward of Joe Layton rehearsing his dancers

Something Very Strange

"SAIL AWAY"

NOËL COWARD

Moderato

This is not a day like an-y oth-er day,

This is some-thing spe-cial and a - part.   Some-thing to re-mem-ber when the

ELAINE STRITCH in "Sail Away"

Why Do The Wrong People Travel?

"SAIL AWAY"

NOËL COWARD

Travel they say improves the mind, An ir - ri - tat - ing
Just when you think ro - mance is ripe It rath - er sharp - ly

plat - i - tude, which frank - ly, en - tre - nous, Is ver - y far from
dawns on you that each sweet ser - e - nade Is for the tour - ist

true. Per - son - al - ly I've yet to find that long - i - tude and
trade. An - y at - trac - tive na - tive type who res - o - lute - ly

REFRAIN (in tempo)

Why do— the wrong peo-ple trav-el, trav-el, trav-el When the
Why do— the wrong peo-ple trav-el, trav-el, trav-el When the
Why do— the wrong peo-ple trav-el, trav-el, trav-el When the

right peo-ple stay back home? _____ What com-pul-sion com-
right peo-ple stay back home? _____ What ex-plains this mass
right peo-ple stay back home? _____ What pe-cu-liar ob-

pels them and who the hell tells them To drag their bags to Zan-zi-bar in-
ma-nia to leave Penn-syl-va-nia And clack a-round like flocks of geese, De-
ses-sions in-spire those pro-ces-sions Of fam-i-lies from Hous-ton, Tex. with

stead of stay-ing qui-et-ly in O-ma-ha? The Taj Ma-hal and the
mand-ing dry mar-ti-nis on the Isles Of Greece? In the small-est street, where the
all those cam-er-as a-round their necks? They will take a train or an

158

FLORENCE HENDERSON and **JOSE FERRER** in *"The Girl Who Came To Supper"*

Here And Now

"THE GIRL WHO CAME TO SUPPER"

NOËL COWARD

Whom can I tell? What can I say? How can I breathe, and not be - tray to ev - 'ry soul I see,_____ What to - day _____ means to me? _____

REFRAIN

Here and now _____ I've a won - der - ful se - cret that

On this mar - vel - ous mag - ic morn - ing, Sud - den -

ly — I know. ___ I'm in love, ___ I a -

dore ev - 'ry mo - ment that's hur - ry - ing by.

Up a - bove ___ there's a love - ly new light in the

London (Is A Little Bit Of All Right)

"THE GIRL WHO CAME TO SUPPER"

Noël Coward

Moderato

I was born and bred in Lon-don, It's the on-ly cit-y I

know. Tho' it's fog-gy and cold and wet, I'd be

zoo, bring a ba - na - na, Feed the ducks in Bat - ter - sea Park or
Row, sit - ting on hors - es. Gros - v'nor Square or Pet - ti - coat Lane, Bel -

take a trip to Kew. It on - ly costs a tan - ner there and
grav - ia, Peck - ham Rye, You can stray thru an - y neigh - bor -

back. Watch our lads in the pal - ace yard
hood. If you have - n't a swank - y club,

Troop the col - or and change the guard and don't for - get your brol - ly and your
Just pop in - to the near - est pub, a lit - tle of what you fan - cy does you

"The Girl Who Came To Supper" (1963) Top, TESSIE O'SHEA sings "London", Below, Coronation scene.

Sir Noël Coward, in a recent interview, was asked his idea of a perfect
life. Without hesitation he replied, "Mine." And a *perfect* tribute to Sir
Noël has been realized in OH, COWARD!, the delightful off-Broadway
revue which opened at the New Theatre, October 4, 1972. The show,
devised and directed by Roderick Cook (who also appears in it), runs the
gamut of Coward's way with words and music, capturing in but two short
hours the true essence and magic of Noël Coward.

WRODERICK PRODUCTIONS PRESENT

BARBARA CASON　　**RODERICK COOK**　　**JAMIE ROSS**

in

A NEW MUSICAL COMEDY REVUE

Words and Music by **NOËL COWARD**

Settings by **HELEN POND** and **HERBERT SENN**
Musical Direction and Arrangements by **RENE WIEGERT**

Production Stage Manager by Jay Leo Colt

Additional Musical Arrangements by Herbert Helbig and Nicholas Deutsch

Devised and Directed by **RODERICK COOK**

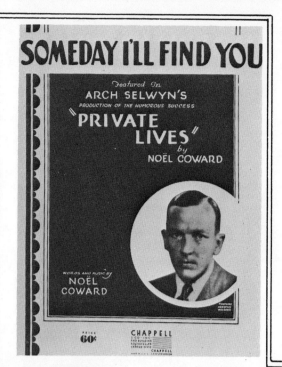

Index Of Songs